MW01706997

The Beautiful Attitudes

The Wisdom Of The Beatitudes

STEPHEN M. CROTTS

CSS Publishing Company, Inc.
Lima, Ohio

THE BEAUTIFUL ATTITUDES

Library of Congress Cataloging-in-Publication

Crotts, Stephen M.
The beautiful attitudes : the wisdom of the Beatitudes / Stephen M. Crotts.
p. cm.
ISBN 0-7880-0717-3 (pbk.)
1. Beatitudes. I. Title.
BT382.C76 1996
241.5'3—dc20 95-39209
CIP

ISBN: 0-7880-0717-3 PRINTED IN U.S.A.

To

William and Sue Hoffman

friends in the truest sense

Contents

1

The Beautiful Attitudes

Matthew 3-7

It's the most famous sermon Jesus ever preached — The Sermon on the Mount.

But just because it is well known does not mean it is well understood, much less well obeyed.

So we begin a study of it in hopes that in the end we can each wrap our flesh around Christ's sermon on the mount and go live it in the world.

As we begin, it is vital to comprehend the context in which Christ preached his message. And here there are four points that must be understood.

Master

The first point is about how Christ chose God the Father.

We know precious little about the first 30 years of Jesus' life. We know he grew in wisdom and in stature, and in favor with God and man. We know that by age 12 Christ understood the Scriptures so well he was able to converse impressively with the elders in the Temple at Jerusalem. And we think his father Joseph died during his teenage years, leaving him the eldest son and thus the breadwinner for his mother Mary and several brothers and sisters. So until he was 30, Christ dutifully ran the carpentry shop and provided for his family.

Then suddenly it was as if Christ Jesus knew the hour had struck. So he put his younger brother James in charge of the shop and set out as an itinerant preacher.

His first stop was Gilgal on the west bank of the Jordan River. There John the Baptist was calling for Israel to repent. And as a symbolic gesture, each who responded passed through the waters of the Jordan River. Jesus himself believed John's message. And he was baptized.

The question is "Why?" Was it for the wishing away of his sins? No, for Christ was sinless.

The answer lies much deeper.

Historically, when Joshua led Israel from Mount Nebo down the Valley of Shittim, they crossed over the Jordan into the Promised Land at Gilgal. Thus the place was not unlike our Plymouth Rock. It was where Israel first came over, where they began as a nation.

Many of the ancient Jewish prophets often called Israel to return to Gilgal, contemplate their God and their behavior, and to renew their fidelity with the covenant.

By going to Gilgal and baptizing, John was saying the old Israel was dead, apostate. And he preached for a new Israel to pass through the Jordan River and become a nation.

Jesus identified with the new Israel. And so he was baptized.

Methods

Now that Christ had chosen God the Father and the new Israel as his master, he next selected his methods of ministry.

Matthew 4 fills in here with the temptation story.

The Spirit led Jesus into the wilderness where our Lord fasted 40 days. Then Satan, ever up to his old tricks, slithered up to try to entice Christ away from God the

Father. Just as he did Eve and Adam, so he will do Christ — get him alone, twist God's word, and even use food as a lure.

Satan sneered, "So you want to serve God? Fine! But look how hungry you are! Turn these stones into bread! That's the ticket! People love food! Feed their bellies and they'll follow you anywhere!" And Jesus said, "Man shall not live by bread alone, but by every word that proceeds from the mouth of God."

Then Satan took Christ to the pinnacle of the Temple. "Jump!" he urged. "Crowds like magic tricks! Surely angels will catch you! That'd really dazzle the crowds! Such showmanship will insure a huge following!" All Christ said was, "Thou shalt not tempt the Lord thy God!"

Finally Satan took Jesus to a high mountain and in a moment of time showed him all the kingdoms of history — Rome, Greece, the czars, England, the USA. "This is mine," Satan preened, "and I give it to whom I will. I'll give it to you if you bow to me!" And Jesus rebuked the devil, saying, "It is written, you shall worship the Lord and Him only shall you serve."

Thus Christ rejected being a materialistic belly-god of bread, a lord of dazzling magic tricks and occult power. First John calls all that the lust of the eyes, the lust of the flesh, and the pride of life. Pleasure. Power. And prestige.

Instead Christ chose the methods of love, of suffering servanthood, of the cross.

The Men

Now that Jesus had selected his master and his methods he set about choosing his men. Matthew 4:18 (and following) tells of our Lord's call to Peter, James,

John, Matthew and Simon the zealot. Twelve in all. None rich. None all that educated or powerful. Mostly fishermen. A few government bureaucrats, some zealots and the like. All notable mostly for their lack of notability.

If I were picking my twelve apostles I'd have selected generals, pop musicians, college professors, a governor and a wealthy banker or two. Yet Christ selected twelve no-names.

Yet, if one looks closely these twelve did have something going for them.

They were available. The Bible says Christ called them and "they left their nets" to follow him.

They were teachable. Unlike the pharisaical know-it-alls, these twelve hadn't made up their minds what they believed yet.

They were faithful. They trusted Christ; Peter trusted enough to actually step out of the boat and walk on water!

And they were responsible. Jesus sent them out in pairs to minister. And each of them was willing to assume such a ministry.

Over the next three years of Christ's ministry these twelve men were to be the primary focus of his work. The multitudes, the lukewarm — they got some of Jesus' attention, but it was the crumbs mostly. For it was these twelve, these faithful, available, responsible and teachable men, who got the bread.

Sad, but in many a minister's priority and scheduling it's the lukewarm and the worldly who devour the most of our time. And this shouldn't be!

We should have time for the multitudes in every week, but every single one of us should be devoted to mentoring a small group of friends, perhaps a spouse, and our children, if the good Lord so blesses us.

The Message

So, Jesus chose his master, his methods, his men. Now he chose his message, the Sermon on the Mount.

It's probably a mistake to call Matthew 5-7 one sermon. Jesus was a better preacher than to over-dazzle an audience with so much light. What the Scriptures record for us in these three chapters is most likely a condensation, a summation of all Jesus taught over a weekend retreat.

Matthew 5:1-12 tells us Christ avoided the crowds and went up in the mountains calling only the twelve to himself. Such behavior should quicken your pulse. For the Lord is God of the mountains — Mount Sinai, Mount Moriah, Mount Carmel, Mount Calvary. When God moves upon a mountain something significant is in the offing!

A cursory reading of Christ's message usually results in astonishment. Many react to the Sermon by calling it unrealistic, idealistic, and unworkable in the real world.

I'm told of a wife who liked to rearrange the household furniture. Her husband came home after a long business trip and found a note on the door: "Warning: New traffic patterns ahead. Stay alert!" This is basically what our Lord says in the Sermon on the Mount. At least six times Jesus says, "You have heard it said, but I say unto you." Love your enemy; go the second mile. When slapped, turn the cheek. Give your cloak to one who asks.

Many read such pronouncements and recoil. "That's insane! No one can live like that!"

But G.K. Chesterton wrote, "The Sermon on the Mount is not a crazy message which our sane world cannot reasonably accept; it is rather absolute sanity preached to a world of lunatics."

One might say it's Jesus' sermon on how to live right-side-up in an upside-down world.

Standing alone, the Beatitudes do seem irrelevant and unrealistic. But contrast Christ's words with their opposites and suddenly the message becomes intensely relevant!

Blessed are the poor in spirit as opposed to the proud, arrogant and self-centered.

Blessed are the mournful as opposed to the indifferent, loveless and jovial.

Blessed are the meek as opposed to the abusive, cocky, overconfident.

Blessed are the hungry and thirsty for righteousness as opposed to the self-satisfied, sneaky and ruthless.

The merciful as opposed to the unkind, unforgiving and harsh.

The pure in heart as contrasted with the guilt-ridden, impure and manipulative.

The peacemakers as opposed to the warmongers, troublemakers and argumentative.

The persecuted for righteousness' sake as opposed to the fence-sitters, cowards and compromisers.

But be quick to notice that after all of this astonishingly peaceful talk, Jesus ends this sermon with a threat: the parable of the wise and foolish builders. "Hear and do what I say and you build on the rock. Hear and do not do my words? You build on sand and the storm will come and wash your life away," Jesus said.

So Jesus chose his master, his methods, his men and his message. And if he didn't say anything else in his Sermon on the Mount, he most certainly said this: You guys are going to be different! He said that in a world of pain we'd stick out, not like a sore thumb, but like a healed thumb! We'd be different in our hunger for what's right, in our generosity, in our humility, in our peacemaking, prayers and enduring quality of life.

What God told Israel in Isaiah 60 he tells us in the Sermon on the Mount: "Arise, shine, for thy light has come and the glory of the Lord has risen upon you. Nations shall come to the brightness of your rising."

Conclusion

A few winters ago I was driving home from the mountains and, along with 200 other cars, got stuck on a mile-long hill that was glazed with ice. We were helpless to move without sliding into the ditch or each other. Suddenly an old, yellow dump truck came up behind us, passed, and began to spread grit and salt on the road. A cheer went up, and within the minute 200 helpless motorists began to find their traction and head home.

"Lord," I prayed, "thank you for that driver in the dump truck. Make me a Christian like that, able to change the very climate of our slippery, dangerous, freezing, helpless world!"

Jesus, I hear what you're saying.
Do thou help me to do it. Amen.

2

Blessed Are The Poor In Spirit

Blessed are the poor in spirit, for theirs is the kingdom of heaven. —Matthew 5:3

Possibly the worst criticism anyone can level at us Christians is to say, "I've watched your life and you're no different than the rest of the world! You're just as greedy, malicious and full of lust as I am!"

Admittedly, sometimes coming to church is like tossing a pebble into a lake. The pebble gets nice and wet on the outside, but the water never penetrates to the inside. Similarly, it's easy to come to church and allow the externals of the Gospel to wash over our outer lives — how we dress, the cut of our hair, our speech, and so forth. But all the while our inner life remains locked up tightly against any penetration by the Gospel. So our conscience, our spirit, our values and our attitudes remain unfazed by truth! And we have a religion of outward show, but it's not life-changing.

Nowhere is the Gospel's lack of penetration more evident than in the Sermon on the Mount. Oliver Wendell Holmes wrote, "Most people are willing to take the Sermon on the Mount as a flag to sail under, but few will use it as a rudder by which to steer."

We come now to the Beatitudes of Jesus, the first words of his most famous sermon. There are eight beatitudes in all. The first four deal with one's relationship with God. The last four deal with one's relationship with people.

Let's immerse ourselves in the first of these eight pronouncements of Jesus. Let's open our inner attitudes to God's beatitudes and find fulfillment in him.

Blessed

First, it is imperative that we understand the formula in which Christ presented the Beatitudes. The traditional English Bible translation reads, "Blessed are the poor in spirit, for theirs is the kingdom of heaven." But there is no "are" in the Greek original. A better translation is: "O the blessedness of the poor in spirit, for theirs is the kingdom of heaven!" Thus the first beatitude is not a simple declarative sentence, but an exclamation. It is an exclamatory remark meant to be shouted with excitement! "O THE BLESSEDNESS OF THE POOR IN SPIRIT . . .!"

The word *blessed* is the word *makarios* in the Greek. It's the same word used for the island of Cyprus in the Mediterranean. Cyprus is known as "the Happy Island." It had it all in Christ's day. The saying was that a person need not go beyond its coastline to find joy. So a fair translation of the first beatitude might be: "O the happiness of the poor in spirit, for theirs is the kingdom of heaven!"

To us moderns happiness means feeling fine. "The wife and I are getting along. The kids are behaving. My investments hit 12 percent last year. And it looks like I'll get that promotion at work!" Do you see how we base our happiness on our circumstances? The trouble with such happiness is that it is so fragile. Why, 90 percent of my life can be going just fine, but 10 percent going poorly can destroy my mood.

This is not the sort of happiness Christ is talking about. The Lord's blessedness or happiness is not what you feel, but what is. Not what is temporary, but what is eternal. Not what you think of your circumstances, but what God thinks.

The Hebrew word for blessed has a word picture behind it — that of a kneeling camel. The idea is that a camel kneels so it can be loaded with silks, spices, treasure and such, then gets up and joins a caravan taking its cargo to distant lands.

This is the picture in Psalm 68:19. "Blessed be the Lord who daily loadeth (or blesses) us with benefits."

So the idea is that a camel is made to be "a ship of the desert." To be blessed, then, is to be like a camel, to be doing that which God put you here to do.

Now, back to the first beatitude. "O the blessedness, of the happy islanders, O the loaded camels carrying treasure, O those happily fulfilled of God . . ." Thus our happiness in God is not a feeling but an abiding fulfillment, not what we think of our circumstances, but what God thinks.

That is the formula in which Jesus presented his beatitudes. Now, this is the first fulfilling attitude.

Poor in Spirit

"O the blessedness of the poor in spirit, for theirs is the kingdom of heaven!"

Do you remember that the first four beatitudes have to do with one's relationship with God? Thus, having an attitude of spiritual poverty is the first principle Christ urges upon his disciples.

This has confused many Christians. Is Christ glorifying poverty? Yes, he is. But it is not physical poverty — lack of food and shelter. Rather, it is spiritual poverty — "poorness in spirit" — that Christ is singling out.

In the Greek, "poor in spirit" means abject poverty, without resources, literally beaten to your knees — being so poor one can only look to God for solace. Thus a literal translation of the first beatitude reads, "O the happiness of the person who realizes his complete spiritual poverty and puts all his trust in God, for his is the kingdom of heaven."

In Luke 18:9 (and following), Jesus told the parable of two men who went into the temple to pray. The first man was rich, proud, and self-righteous. He was a Pharisee. He stood in the most prominent place in the temple and preened like a peacock! Jesus said he "prayed thus with himself." He was not talking to God, but indulging in a kind of inner dialogue of self-congratulation. "I thank thee, Lord of heaven, that I am not like other men — adulterers, liars and thieves. I pray five times a day, fast and tithe."

The second man, a socially despised tax collector, hid in the shadows of the temple. He wouldn't even lift up his eyes to heaven! Rather he beat his breast and anguished in prayer, "Lord, have mercy on me, a sinner!"

I like to say the first man had one eye on himself, one eye on his neighbor, and no eye on God. The second man, however, had one eye on himself, and one eye on God. And in comparing his character with the nature of God, he came away feeling poor and humble.

Jesus said the poor man went down to his house "justified," while the proud man went away "unjustified."

We've a saying here in North Carolina — "high and dry." And it translates into this spiritual truth: high in ego, dry spiritually; high in pride, low with God; high in self, shriveled and dry in spirit and soul.

Do you want an example of this? Revelation 3:17 (and following) describes the church at Laodicia as very wealthy in education, material things and social status, but very impoverished in the things of the Spirit. "You say, 'I am rich; I have acquired wealth and do not need a thing.' But you do not realize that you are wretched, pitiful, poor, blind, and naked." There you have it. High and dry. The more self-righteous we are, the less God-conscious we are.

One way we can tell we're growing spiritually is when we get more Calvinistic. By that I mean when we have a higher view of God and a lower view of self; a higher sense of God's sovereignty; a lower sense of one's own plans. God's glory becomes everything. My own glory becomes marginal. I become more concerned with being faithful than with being fruitful. Or, in short, I become convinced of my own utter poverty and yet become aware of God's incredible riches.

As the hymn writer puts it, "Nothing in my hand I bring, simply to the cross I cling."

Jesus is saying that the disciples' relationship with God begins with a realization that there isn't one. And it continues from there with an ever deepening understanding that only God is great. I am nothing. God is rich. I am poor.

It is helpful to study the apostle Paul here. When we first meet him in Scripture he is a religious Pharisee strutting and preening himself in public, crowing self-righteously. Then he meets Jesus and quickly becomes singularly unimpressed with himself, while becoming overwhelmed with God's glory.

In A.D. 58, he writes, "Paul an apostle — not from men nor through man, but through Jesus Christ" (Galatians 1:1).

In A.D. 63 he writes, "The saying is sure, and worthy of full acceptance, that Christ Jesus came into the world to save sinners. And I am the chief of sinners."

Note Paul did not say "I *was* the chief of sinners." Poor in spirit, Paul says, "I *am* the chief of sinners."

The closer we get to God the more amazing his grace is. The more we realize all he is, the more we recognize all we are not. "Nothing in my hand I bring, simply to the cross I cling!" Oh, Lord, it all depends on you!

Conclusion

Perhaps there is one of you reading this who has not known such truth. You have tried to establish your relationship with God by your own works. You've become devoutly religious. In the observance of rules you think you will earn your way back to God. Now you think you are better than others. Yet really on the inside you are tired, hard and joyless.

You have one eye on yourself, one eye on your neighbor and no eye on God. And you are unjustified.

Good news! "O the blessedness of those who realize their complete spiritual poverty with God, theirs is the kingdom of God!"

Perhaps today you would look into the splendor of God and find your own raggedness. And kneeling like a camel, you'd ask God to load you with his rich grace.

Lord, have mercy on me, a sinner.
For Jesus' sake. Amen.

3

Blessed Are Those Who . . . *What?*

Blessed are those who mourn, for they shall be comforted — Matthew 5:4

I remember New Year's Day. The sadness. A gnawing ache. A restlessness. A deep sense of dissatisfaction. "Maybe you're just tired," I said to myself. "A touch depressed. Why don't you get some extra sleep, go see a funny movie, call an old friend, get lost in a book."

After all, I've been there before. I know what to do! When feeling depressed, if all else fails, read a good biography. You'll find out others had lives that weren't all that easy. John Wesley struggled in a difficult marriage. Robert Frost was past 40 when his first poem was published. George Fredrick Handel went bankrupt twice. This is life! This is the way living really is! It was then, is now, and ever shall be until Jesus comes!

Another ploy I use when down is to count my blessings. Let's see, 21 years of marriage to Kathryn. She's not only my best friend, but I get to take a long walk with her almost every day. Three growing, healthy children, all Christians. Good health. I don't think I missed a single day of work last year. The opportunity to preach on college campuses and impact a future generation. Four days of scenery and snow skiing in New Hampshire like you wouldn't believe! A book accepted by a publisher. A chance to write for three national magazines. Being a part of a fine local church with all her love and joy and challenge. Fixing up an old stone house to live in. Getting to sit at the controls of an F-16 fighter jet. Piloting over the Grand Canyon. The adventure of exploring and preaching across Bermuda. Driving around in an old but restored 1968 Mustang (even though the heater does not work!).

So I said to myself, "Shouldn't that be about enough?" Still I wasn't perking up. So I quoted Shakespeare to myself, the old priest's advice to Juliet, "A pack of blessings rests on your head, but thou, like a sullen and pouting wench, frowneth upon thy fortune!"

"Maybe you're just greedy," I mused. "You expect too much. You're just another overly ambitious preacher!"

"Or maybe," I feared, "it's repetition depression." You know. Last year was so wonderful, but can I do it again next year? Will there be more joy, more love, more faithfulness?

Still my spirits were low. So I sat down and seriously asked myself, "Just what is it you want, Stephen?" A new car? No. Another house? No. A boat? No. A fancy trip? No. A job that's different? No. New friends? No.

What I want is God. I don't want to sin anymore. I want the Bridegroom to come. I don't want to have to look on human wreckage anymore. I want God's kingdom to come. I want to go to heaven. I want to look upon the face of Jesus.

No. I'm not suicidal. It's just a yearning, an unfulfilled longing, a grieving in my soul.

I'm not the only one who feels this way. I was having lunch with a businessman. He is one of those humans who has it all together — faith, spouse, children, career, looks, health, income. We had a deep, brooding conversation for 45 minutes and he confessed quite honestly, "I wonder what it'd be like to be really happy for ten minutes."

Jesus had a word about all this in his Sermon on the Mount. "Blessed are they that mourn, for they shall be comforted." The notion of mourning in this beatitude means grief or weeping or sadness. But it means more than crying over the death of a loved one. It also includes mourning over sinfulness, grief over loss of innocence, the sorrow of repentance. It is to feel the hurt God feels when he looks out over a sinful world.

The best translation of this passage is: "O the fulfillment of the unfulfilled. O the happiness of the unhappy." In the English language we recognize such a statement as oxymoronic. That's like "pretty ugly" or "rush hour" or "tax simplification." Two notions that don't belong together are oxymoronic. But still Jesus utters his second beatitude: "O the blessedness of those who let God break their hearts with the things that break his heart. O the happiness of them that care, that feel, that cry over sin. They shall be comforted."

Some think the Christian life is all smiles, that we should try to be bubbly in the spirit every moment of every day. But such an attitude flies in the face of Christ's second beatitude. It is more in keeping with the world's character than it is with God.

For the world says, "Blessed are those who don't care, who don't get involved, the partygoers, the flippant, the high, those who insulate themselves, who live life in the fast lane, who go where the good is."

But Jesus said, "O the fulfillment, the blessedness, the joy of those who care, who mourn, because God is going to bring in the day of comfort."

Did it ever occur to you that it is a sin to get too comfortable in this sinful, rebellious, and hurting world?

In Ezekiel 9 the Lord observed the wickedness of his people. And he commanded his angels, "Go through the land and put a mark on the foreheads of all those who sigh and groan over sin. Then draw your sword and kill the rest! And begin at the temple!"

Christ knew how to sigh and groan. He wept at John's funeral. He lamented Lazarus' passing. He cried over Jerusalem.

The psalmist wrote, "My eyes shed streams of tears, because men do not keep thy law" (Psalm 119:136).

In Philippians 3:18, Paul confessed, "For many, of whom I have often told you and now tell you even with tears, live as enemies of the cross of Christ."

Where is it one finds this sort of authentic sin-grief in our world today? In Durham, North Carolina, a jury was gathered to hear a case involving a brutal murder. A female juror, hearing the horrid details of drugs, rape, and homicide, was so overcome with the pain of it all she began to weep. She finally had to be dismissed,

I like that. For we today are far too calloused when we can look upon drunkenness, divorce, abuse, murder, lying, greed, Sabbath breaking, and theft and never once feel so much as a twinge of heartache.

I see this beautiful attitude in the life and art of Vincent van Gogh, a turn-of-the-century Dutch impressionist painter. As a young Christian van Gogh sought ordination to the ministry. Since his education was inadequate, the only license to preach he could obtain was through a missionary society which sent him into the Belgian coal fields. Here were the poorest of the poor. And van Gogh lived among them. He ate their food, shared their clothing, and preached his heart out.

The missions society, upon checking on him, found him to have become as starved, dirty, and ragged as his miners. He was fired for being an unfit reflection on the society.

Van Gogh began to paint out his grief. He used his canvas to show the world the face of coal miners and their abused plight. Over the next 20 years he finished 2,000 pictures.

Not one sold during his lifetime. Lonely, overlooked, unloved, some say van Gogh went insane. He shot himself and died two days later in a rented flat above a pool hall in France. His body was placed on a pool table. Many of his paintings were hung on the walls of the hall. He was laid to rest in obscurity.

My favorite van Gogh painting is titled, *Starry Night Over The Rhone*. The viewer is on the shore of a lake. It is night and across the water is a town, the lights of a party revealing happy couples making merry. Yet there is a cold, dark gulf separating the viewer from the fun. A feeling of isolation sweeps over you. But in the sky! Oh the sky! The stars burn brightly, like torches, lending a sense of hope from above.

Folk singer Don McClean wrote a song about van Gogh in which he laments: "For they could not love you, but still your love was true. And when no hope was left inside on that starry, starry night, you took your life as lovers often do. But I could have told you, Vincent, this world was never meant for one as beautiful as you."

I also see this godly grief in my friend, Jim. He and his wife were unable to have children of their own. So they adopted. A three-week-old baby girl was placed in their loving arms. They named her Joy. And together they set out to make a happy life. But as the child grew it became apparent something was seriously wrong. Short attention span, volatile emotions, learning disabled — all the symptoms of fetal alcohol syndrome. Evidently Joy's mom had drunk way too much alcohol during pregnancy and damaged the child. So Joy will always struggle. She'll never have the life she should have. And Jim mourns.

A juror at a murder trial, a Dutch impressionist painter, an adoptive parent. They all teach us that some things in life are so awful that the only way we can handle them is by weeping. And when we weep, we find God with us.

Isaiah 53:3 describes Jesus as "a man of sorrows, and acquainted with grief."

There is a legend in Jewish folklore about "Lamed-Van-Tzaddkim." He is one of the ten righteous men by whose merit God allows the world to continue.

Recall Genesis 19:16-33. The two angels have set out to destroy Sodom and Gomorrah. Abraham greets them and invites them in for a meal, and learning of their mission pleads, "If you find ten righteous men in the city, will you show mercy?" The angels agree.

According to rabbinical legend there was but one righteous man in Sodom. For many years he'd lived, taught, prayed, and encouraged his city to God. His labors were met only with scorn.

Still he begged his listeners to turn to God.

One day as he walked the streets of Sodom a child asked, "Poor stranger, why do you live here weeping and teaching us? You spend yourself body and soul, but can't you see it's hopeless?"

To which the righteous man replied, "When I first came here I thought I could change people. Now I know I can't. But if I keep crying and caring and praying I can at least keep them from changing me."

"O the happiness of the unhappy. O the fulfillment of the unfulfilled. O the blessedness of those who mourn, who let God break their hearts with what breaks his. O the joy of those who care, who weep, who can still feel. They shall be comforted, soothed, healed, requited."

I point out that there are large groups of Christians who promise to remove your grief. Some charismatics pledge to you a prosperity, an overflowing, so that you'll always live life on the peak.

Then there are some fundamentalists who look at mourning and say, "Buck it up! Pray harder. Do right. Open your Bible! There's no use feeling sad!"

And there's the self-help book shelf at the Christian book store. Just fix yourself with a good read like *You Can Be Joyous Everyday!* or *Blow Away the Dark Clouds of Depression Forever!* But I don't want my grief removed by anyone but Jesus!

Soon. So soon, my sisters and brothers! In that great getting up morning, fare thee well, fare thee well!

No more obesity! No more unemployment. No more scorn. No more cancer. No more alcoholism.

Arthritis? Gone forever! Loneliness? Vanquished! Old age? No more! Sin? History! Pain? A bygone! Rejection? A thing of the past! Death? Swallowed up in life!

What will it be like, then, to wake from sleep refreshed and find life an endless, pristine celestial morning? What will it be like to raise an arm and find it strong, youthful and new again? What will it be like on that distant shore to look into a mirror and see one's own face without wrinkles, fatigue, worry, the ravages of time? What will it be like to look into the face of an old friend and see perfect companionship? What will it be like to stand and look on the face of Jesus, to be cuddled in his arms and have him wipe away every teardrop? What will it be like when we're comforted and can sing new songs of Zion without distraction, without hypocrisy, without the static of our feeble flesh?

Behold, I hear the voice of God say, "Now the dwelling place of God is with men . . . There will be no more death or mourning or crying or pain ... I am making all things new!" (Revelation 21).

And the church says, "Even so, Lord, come!"

All of this God has taught me since New Year's Day. It's okay to feel sadness, to have unfulfilled longings, to grieve.

To do so is normal in a world like ours. It might not change anything. But it will surely keep the world from changing you.

"O the blessed fulfillment of those who mourn. They shall be comforted."

Lord, let me feel as you feel,
care as you care, mourn as you mourn.
And on that day may I receive your comfort. Amen.

4

The Beautiful Attitude Of Humility

Blessed are the meek, for they shall inherit the earth — Matthew 5:5

The way of God's kingdom is opposite our modern way. We say, "Blessed are the self-righteous, those who don't lean on God, those who have it all together." Jesus says, "Blessed are the poor in spirit, those who realize their absolute spiritual poverty."

We say, "Blessed are those who laugh it up, who party down, who don't care, who won't be bothered." Jesus says, "Happy are the unhappy, who let God break their hearts with what breaks his."

The world says, "Blessed are the tough, overbearing intimidators who know how to get their way, the arrogant, the proud." Christ intones, "Blessed are the meek, for they shall inherit the earth."

Of all Jesus' beatitudes this one is the most antithetical, the most absurd, the hardest to swallow. "Aw, come on, Jesus! The wimps shall inherit the earth? Me be a doormat? Me let people ride roughshod over me? You've got to be kidding! What is this? Some sort of invitation to become a weakling, to be ignored?"

Years ago I was digging in my garden and accumulated a wheelbarrow full of extra dirt. "What am I going to do with all this earth?" I wondered. My child said, "Dad, why don't we give it to the meek?"

Comedian Jerry Clower played football for Mississippi. Their opening game was with Baylor, a Baptist college. To get ready for the contest Clower jogged, practiced, and didn't miss prayer meeting for six weeks. On the game day, first play from scrimmage, Clower got walloped. His helmet flew off and he hit the dirt face first. He jumped up sputtering and complaining to his opponent, "I thought you were supposed to be a Christian, and see what you did to me?!" The lineman smiled and said, "Sure, I'm a Christian. The Bible says, 'The meek shall inherit the earth,' and I was just helping you get your share."

Then there's the one about the man who died and went to heaven. Standing in front of the pearly gates, he noticed two signs. The first one read, "All men who were henpecked by their wives stand in this line." To no one's amazement the line had 234 men in it. The second sign read, "All men who weren't henpecked stand in this line." One man waited there. Now Peter came out, looked at the first line, smiled knowingly, then did a double take at the solitary man in line two. "Excuse me, did you read that sign?" "Yes." "You mean to tell me you weren't henpecked?" "Oh, my wife told me to stand in this line!"

Meekness. We've turned it into a joke.

We've more in common with Soviet Premier Nikita Khrushchev, who on a 1950s visit to a French cathedral said, "There is much in Christ that is in common with us communists, but I cannot agree with him when he says when you are hit on the right cheek, turn the left cheek. I believe in another principle. If I am hit on the left cheek I hit back on the right cheek so hard the head might fall off!" To which we all say a hearty "Amen!"

Let us study the third of Christ's beautiful attitudes. The three points we'll look at are: meekness, how it is applied to our relationship with God, and how it is applied to our relationship with people.

What It Means

"Blessed are the meek." The original Greek word for *meek* is *praus*. It translates as gentle, humble, considerate and courteous.

Meekness does not mean weak-willed, wimpy or devoid of courage. Rather, it means self-controlled. In Canada they have these huge Clydesdale horses which can be hitched up to pull great logs out of the forest for timber companies. These horses are so strong yet so gentle that little children can crawl all over them and play about their hooves without injury. This is a picture of meekness, of tamed strength. It is mayhem and manners in perfect control.

In Matthew 11:29, Jesus described himself as "gentle and lowly in heart." It is the same word: *praus*. God in human flesh: tamed strength able to heal blindness, coddle little children, raise the dead, wear a crown of thorns, feed 5,000, hang upon a cross, yet slay the wicked with the breath of his mouth.

In 2 Corinthians 10:1 the apostle Paul refers to both Jesus and himself as meek. You will understand that the Corinthian church was a mess. They didn't respect their elders. The authority of Scripture was rejected. Anarchy reigned supreme. So Paul visited them. But he came meekly. He wrote, "By the meekness and gentleness of Christ, I appeal to you — I, Paul who am timid when face to face with you, but bold when away."

So, the best understood translation of the third beatitude? "O the blessedness, O the happy fulfillment of the gentle, the humble, the considerate, the courteous! O the blessed meek, those of tamed strength, they shall inherit the earth."

The question arises, how does one develop this attitude in his life? I mean, humility is a hard quality! As soon as you say you've got it, you've lost it. "Don't you people understand just what an all-around good fellow of absolute humility I am?" "Perhaps you've read my book, *Humility and How I Attained It,* $39.95 at your local bookstore." "Last year the deacons gave me the humility award badge but they had to take it back because I kept wearing it." See what I mean?

How does humility come? Just bow your head and grunt prayerfully, "I will be humble. I will be humble. I will be humble!"?

Look at the logical progression of the beatitudes. "Blessed are the poor in spirit." A disciple's relationship with God begins by recognizing I am bankrupt morally and spiritually. I am totally dependent upon God's mercy.

The second attitude is mourning. I am spiritually impoverished and I care. I cry over it. I can feel God's hurt over this writhing, sinful world.

Third comes meekness. Because of my poverty and grief, I've no room for pride, for arrogance and a sense of having arrived.

So how do I become humble? First, I gain a true estimate of who God is. Then, second, I gain a true estimate of who I am by comparison. When I do that I don't have any trouble being humble.

Meekness With God

That is something of what it means to be meek. Now this: meekness in our relationship with God.

Five hundred years ago Martin Luther observed, "God created the world out of nothing. As long as you're not yet anything, God cannot make something out of you."

As a Christian I must recognize God as eternal, almighty, holy and loving.

I also recognize God as my creator. I am dust. My life span is but a few years. And I shall return to dust. I am neither very strong nor intelligent. There is sin in my life. I don't love very well. So I am poor in spirit and I mourn.

This keeps me humble. It kills pride.

All this, yet it is so easy to lose sight of these things and become impressed with myself. Why, some good looks, a career, money, a new car, a few accolades and I can become so impressed with myself that I forget God.

2 Chronicles 26 is a case in point. King Uzziah's life is spread out before us there. God blessed Uzziah with a godly, two-parent home. His father was a king who "did what was right in the eyes of the Lord." He was crowned at age 16. The nation unified behind him. He enjoyed excellent health. Zechariah the prophet guided him. He was a builder. He won his battles. His standing army was huge and well-trained. His fame and power grew. He ruled 52 years.

But in verse 16 it says, "After Uzziah became powerful his pride led to his downfall."

Did you hear about the woodpecker pecking on a tree when a lightning bolt struck? He got up and congratulated himself, saying, "Boy, I didn't know I had it in me!"

Uzziah's name means, "God is my help." He forgot that and became vain. And the Bible says one day he strolled into the temple, picked up a censer, and prepared to make an offering. Eighty-one priests opposed him. That was their job. God had strictly prescribed how he was to be worshipped. And Levite priests were to handle the liturgy. But Uzziah swept them aside. "I'll do it myself," he said.

Uzziah was sort of like Michael Jordan, who conquered basketball and then went after baseball. Uzziah had conquered armies, built cities, and marshalled the masses. He now thinks he can do anything, even come to God on his own terms.

So there he stood in the temple, censer in hand, raging at the 81 priests who opposed him, when suddenly, leprosy broke out on his forehead. And the Bible says the priests didn't have to show Uzziah the door for "he himself was eager to leave because the Lord had afflicted him."

Uzziah spent the rest of his life as a leper remembering that only God is great.

Scripture is full of swell-heads who think they are something, but learn the hard way that God is God and we are not.

Acts 12 tells of King Herod accepting worship from his subjects. An angel smote him, his guts spilt and worms ate him.

Daniel 4 tells of Nebuchadnezzar, whom God made great. Walking on his palace roof he surveyed his realm and said, "Is this not the great Babylon I have built ... by my mighty power ... for my glorious majesty?" He was smitten with madness and lived like a wild dog for many months.

I remind you that it's not just ancient history in which God opposes the proud. It still occurs in modern times. For years the Soviet Union said, "There is no God!" Even Russian cosmonauts sneered, "I went into the heavens and I didn't see God there." Finally, when God had enough, he said, "There is no Soviet Union!"

Lord Byron's poem, "The Destruction of Sennacherib," has this in it. 2 Kings 18-19 tells of the Assyrian king Sennacherib of Ninevah. He wrote boastfully of himself that he was "king of the universe." But when he attacked Israel and mocked God, an angel unsheathed his sword and in one night slew 185,000 Assyrian soldiers. Sennacherib retreated to Ninevah and was himself assassinated by his two sons. Lord Byron tells the story.

The Assyrians came down like the wolf on the fold,
And his cohorts were gleaming in purple and gold;
And the sheen of their spears was like stars on the sea,
When the blue wave rolls nightly on deep Galilee.
For the angel of death spread his wings on the blast,
And breathed in the face of the foe as he passed.
And the eyes of the sleepers waxed deadly and chill,
And their hearts but once heaved, and forever grew still.
And there lay the steed with his nostril all wide,
But through it there rolled not the breath of his pride:
And the foam of his gasping lay white on the turf,
And cold as the spray of the rock-beating surf.
And there lay the rider distorted and pale,
And with the dew on his brow and the rust on his mail.
And the tents were all silent, the banners alone,
The lances unlifted, the trumpet unblown.
And the widows of Ashur are loud in their wail,
And the idols are broke in the temple of Baal;
And the might of the gentiles, unsmote by the sword,
Hath melted like snow in the glance of the Lord.

"Blessed are the meek, for they shall inherit the earth." Is it beginning to make sense?

So far we have sought to uncover the meaning of meekness and study it on one's relation to God. Now let's study . . .

Meekness Before Man

Numbers Chapter 12 tells of Moses leading Israel out of Egyptian slavery into the wilderness. Miriam wanted some of the glory. And being a hard-driving, high-achieving woman, she opposed Moses. "Does God speak only through Moses?" Rather than backhanding her, verse three says, "Now Moses was a very humble man, more humble than anyone on the face of the earth." He invited Miriam to the tent of meeting to lay her case before the Lord. There God came in a pillar of fire, reaffirmed Moses' leadership, and Miriam was suddenly afflicted with leprosy! What does Moses do? What would you have done? "Ha, ha! You had it coming! That'll teach you to oppose me!" No. Moses would have none of this. He simply prayed for Miriam's healing. And it was so. That's meekness. Tamed strength.

I know of a meek grandmother. Her daughter-in-law is a feminist, humanist, egotistical know-it-all. When she visits with her husband and two children she is totally domineering, arrogant and disruptive.

It'd be easy to use your power to mash her, to drive her away in the heat of well-deserved righteous indignation. But if you're a Christian woman wanting to see your son, your grandchildren, and daughter-in-law ever again, meekness is your only recourse. So this woman practices humility, servanthood, and lets her life speak for 12 years now. And the impact is amazing. Over the years the daughter-in-law is mellowing. She's going back to church. She doesn't have all the answers. And what's more, she's still coming for visits.

Remember when the New Testament was being written? Nero was emperor of Rome. And he was rich, iron-fisted, and cruel. He burned the slums of Rome to build it better. And he blamed the fire on Christians, then severely persecuted them.

The apostle Paul was preaching at the same time. He was poor, rejected by his own people, meekly trying to sort out the problems of the Corinthian church. Paul was arrested and eventually beheaded by Nero. Two thousand years later we call our sons Paul and our dogs Nero. Indeed! The meek do inherit the earth.

Visit the Vatican in Rome. The baptistry rests upon a beautiful slab of red jasper. It's Emperor Trajan's coffin lid. Trajan was one of the worst persecutors of the early church. But he died and was buried along with his empire. Yet the church of Jesus lives on! The Vatican has dumped Trajan's body and commandeered his rich casket lid. And new converts stand atop the grave of the proud as they are baptized into the faith!

In 1985 the church sent me to South Texas to do a Fellowship of Christian Athletes youth retreat — the junior high variety. Now everyone should spend a week at a junior high retreat. The hysterics, the energy, the noise — who says there is no purgatory?

A junior high student's idea of fun is picking on other people. And Bruce was their focus for the week. Bruce had cerebral palsy. He walked with jerks and spoke awkwardly. You guessed it — the kids spent their week imitating Bruce's awkwardness and mimicking his speech.

I was angry. I taught on self-esteem, the goodness of God's creation. And I talked to the leaders personally, trying to get them to desist.

You can imagine my anger when I found out the students had asked Bruce to give the devotional in our last assembly. Bruce jerked his way to the podium and it took him five minutes to speak nine words. "I . . . love . . . Jesus . . . Christ . . . and . . . Jesus . . . Christ . . . loves . . . me!" When he finished there was dead silence except for the wind blowing across the prairie and into the chapel filled with 400 kids. Then someone started to cry, and revival broke out. Until way past midnight kids were coming to the open mike to repent, to ask forgiveness, to give their hearts to Jesus.

I still walk into Christian Athletes conferences and campus meetings and nearly grown men say, "Remember me? I was at the South Texas camp with you and Bruce. That's when I gave my heart to the Lord!"

I tell you, it wasn't good preaching or music or discipline that won those kids over. It was Bruce's meekness.

Conclusion

"O the happy fulfillment of the meek, they shall inherit the earth."

In the south of Egypt half-buried in the sand is a broken statue of a sneering pharaoh. Carved into the base is the inscription, "My name is Ozymandias, king of kings: Look on my works, ye mighty and despair." Nothing else remains except a trackless desert waste.

My friend, only God is great! Remember this and be meek.

Hide me, O my Jesus, in the shadow
of your wing, for I know my place. Amen.

5

Happy The Hungry Hearts!

Blessed are those who hunger and thirst for righteousness, for they shall be satisfied. — Matthew 5:6

Search as you might, you will not find the word "beatitude" in the Scriptures. It is rather a word theologians assign to eight sayings of Jesus, the first eight sentences of the Sermon on the Mount. "Beatitude" means "a state of utmost bliss, the highest fulfillment."

We each want this bliss. Witness how we strive for it materially — clothes, cars, trips, looks, job, house. Bliss comes in the next purchase! That's the problem with materialistic bliss. As a local farmer put it, "Worldly riches are like nuts. Many a clothes torn in gathering them. Many a tooth broken in breaking them. But never a belly full in eating them."

In their quest for bliss, others turn to the irrational — alcohol or drugs. This is a quick fix, a chemically-induced euphoria.

Then there are those who seek refuge in fantasy. Take for example the romance novel. Before the American Civil War, Robert E. Lee was an Army officer on post out west. He wrote his wife with concerns about his children's education, giving detailed instructions. "Let him never touch a novel. They print beauty more charming than nature, and describe happiness that never exists. They will teach him to sigh after that which has no reality, to despise the littl egood that is granted us in this world and to expect more than is given."

So it is in one's quest for fulfillment, we stretch our hands out for things, for some narcotic, or even yearn through romance novels. All this, and we're still unfulfilled.

In the beatitudes Jesus gives us the aim and the proper attitudes which bring ultimate bliss. In the first three beatitudes we are told being poor in spirit, mourning, and meekness start us off in our relationship with God. Now, in the fourth beatitude, Jesus says, "Blessed are those who hunger and thirst after righteousness, for they shall be satisfied."

What It Means

Words never exist in isolation. They have a context on the printed page as well as in history. When Jesus discussed "hunger and thirst" he did so in a day when there was no corner grocery store, no faucet to twist to draw water, nor any refrigerator in which to store food. By far, the major portion of the population earned low wages, barely enough for today's food needs. It was what we call today a "hand-to-mouth existence." With no stockpiles of food a famine or theft could lead quickly to starvation.

I've read stories of travelers by camel caravan who were trapped in a sandstorm. Unable to see, they hunkered down in the desert, wrapped themselves in their cloaks, and waited it out. Some storms lasted for days! The travelers ran out of food and water, and when the storm ended, the group crawled out of the desert, more dead than alive.

Such persons had only two things on their minds: Food! Water!

When Jesus said, "Blessed are those who hunger and thirst," he was not describing a genteel hunger, a mere urge to nibble, a craving for a snack. He was describing the hunger of a starving man, the thirst of a desperate man.

Thus, this fourth beatitude asks the questions, "How much do you want God? Is there an intense desperation in your appetite for Christ? Do you only nibble at Jesus, or is it your only desire to gulp him all down?"

There is, furthermore, in this beatitude an oddity in the Greek grammar. The sentence doesn't just read, "O the happy fulfillment of the man who is ravenously hungry and thirsty for righteousness." It says more.

I may say, "I want a piece of bread and a sip of that drink." Or I may explain, "I'm so hungry I want the whole pitcher and the entire loaf of bread!" The latter is what Jesus said in the beatitude. There is in the phraseology a sense of craving the entirety. "Blessed is the man with an overpowering hunger and thirst for all of God's righteousness."

Contrast such a mind-set with today's lukewarm attitude toward God.

When Andrew Young's daughter graduated from college she decided to live in Africa as a missionary. Her daddy hugged her good-bye and complained, "Baby, I just wanted you to have enough religion to be respectable, not enough to go to the poorest continent and be a missionary."

If we're honest, most of us would pray, "Dear God, I'd like to buy a $2 bag of Jesus. Just enough to be saved, but not enough to make me stand out in a crowd. Enough to go to heaven, but not enough to get really involved, if you know what I mean. I just want $2 worth. Enough to make me a Christian: loved, respected, well-treated, and comfortable. This small bag full, please, so I can keep it in my pocket and have a little taste when I please."

Yet this fourth beatitude will have none of that! It insists on the prayer, "God, I want all of you! Now! I'm desperate! Please!"

So, how does one best translate the fourth beatitude? "O the blessedness, O the happy fulfillment of those who are ravenously hungry, who'll just die unless they're fed the whole of God's righteousness. They shall be satisfied!"

Logical Progression

In the first four beatitudes, one finds a sort of logical progression.

The first one teaches that a disciple's relationship with God begins with poverty, a sense of one's lack of everything which pleases God.

Some there are who recognize this about themselves but fail to care. I've had hard-bitten businessmen say to me, "Stephen, I don't know a thing about religion, God, or the Bible. And I don't care! I've more important things to pursue!"

The disciple, however, recognizes his spiritual poverty and mourns over it. He cares. He learns to feel as God feels.

And this leads to the third beatitude — meekness. The disciple is not proud, but teachable, humble, willing to be helped.

Now we come to the fourth beautiful attitude — that of spiritual questing. The disciple sees God's offer of imputed righteousness and hungers and thirsts after the whole of it.

These four attitudes are like an avalanche. A small piece of snow and ice breaks off atop a mountain and begins to tumble downward, gathering momentum as it goes, until there is a veritable crescendo of thundering snow sweeping away all in its path. Likewise, poorness tumbles into mourning which tumbles into meekness and soon one has an irresistible hunger and thirst for Jesus consuming his life and sweeping away all obstacles to the knowledge of God.

What It Looks Like

In Psalm 42, the poet prays, "As a deer pants for the water, so my soul longs after you, O God. My soul thirsts for God, for the living God. Where can I go and meet with God?" The Hebrew word for *pant* is *awrag,* meaning "to breathe heavily after." It did not escape the notice of the ancients that when a man and woman fell in love and embraced, they began to pant, to breathe deeply. Hence, their word for love and pant were much the same. So, "as a deer loves the waters, or breathes heavily after the waters, so my soul pants after thee, O God!"

Hunters used to take advantage of this situation and lie in wait for deer at watering holes. A deer's single-mindedness for water coupled with its heavy breathing made him less vigilant. He'd walk right into danger just to get water.

This has the Gospel in it. John 3:16 says, "God so loved the world" (so breathed heavily after us) "that he gave his only Son." He didn't even see the danger of the cross, he wanted us so!

And, as God loves us he asks that we love him in return.

Certainly there is not much panting after God in our society today. Oh, we breathe heavily after sex or money or fun or more, bigger, newer things. But when it comes to Jesus our culture suffers what Robert Louis Stevenson called "the malady of not wanting."

Thankfully, I have seen such hunger and thirst for God from time to time.

I remember Beverly. She was 19, unmarried, and pregnant. Her boyfriend was insanely jealous and abusive. Beverly came to the church to talk over what choices she still had, became a Christian, and for months afterward just couldn't get enough of worship, scriptures, and fellowship. I well recall a cold, rainy winter Sunday when attendance was low. There Beverly sat in the front row and she was soaking wet! It seems her car wouldn't start, so she'd wrapped her baby in her raincoat and walked one-and-a-half miles to church!

When I first moved to Burlington I sat down with the elders and the people and we debated when we as a church were going to meet and why. The issue of a Sunday night Bible study came up. It would mean more work, more time and energy. It was pointed out that most churches had long ago quit their Sunday evening meetings. Yet someone pointed out if we had a night Bible study we could all grow twice as fast in our understanding of Scripture. So we called the meeting. And for 15 years I've watched many in that crowd come regularly, bringing their Bibles, pens and paper, and hungry minds. This when they could be out boating or watching television!

Some years ago I preached during spiritual emphasis week at Messiah College in Pennsylvania. Young students came to Messiah from all across the nation and even some foreign countries. A young man from the rural poverty of Bolivia was there. Carlos was his name. I watched him the first time he walked into the library. An expression of awe filled his face. "You mean I can read all these books for free?" The librarian assured Carlos it was so. Carlos immediately sat down and said eagerly, "Well, I'm ready! Please bring me the first one!"

Well, these are just a few pictures of true hungering and thirsting after righteousness I've seen over the years.

But what is "righteousness"? The Old Testament prophet Hosea best explains what it is. It seems Hosea was concerned about God's people. They'd lost their zeal for God and were panting like harlots after other idols, things, and themselves. The result was bad behavior.

Hosea diagnosed the problem as twofold. One: There was no knowledge of God among the people. Wise in worldly ways, they were ignorant of truth. "My people are destroyed for lack of knowledge" (Hosea 4:6).

Two: Since there was no knowledge of God, there was no acknowledgment of God. What there was was bad behavior — lying, theft, adultery, greed, murder, idolatry, and so forth. "Their deeds do not permit them to return to their God. For the spirit of harlotry is within them, and they know not the Lord" (Hosea 5:4).

What is unrighteousness? Not knowing and not acknowledging God in one's behavior. What is righteousness? Knowing God and acknowledging him in one's behavior.

Conclusion

I've a friend who is a college president. He tells me that anyone who becomes a Christian and joins a good church and attends it with a hungry attitude for 40 years will have gained the equivalent of ten college educations.

Think of it! If you are hungry for God just look at the banquet he has spread before you in his church! Within these walls are tapes, small groups, videos, fellowships, concerts, books and worship events.

Here one may learn history, music, conflict resolution, loyalty, ethics, joy, sorrow, poetry, theology, but most of all — Jesus Christ! It's a never-ending adventure open to all who consider themselves as not yet having arrived.

Lord, make me hungry for you.
For all of you! And satisfy me with yourself.
For Christ's sake. Amen.

6

The Beautiful Attitude Of Mercy

Blessed are the merciful, for they shall obtain mercy
— Matthew 5:7

General Omar Bradley of World War II fame, in his last speech at West Point, lamented, "This country has many men of science, too few men of God; it has grasped the mystery of the atom, but rejected the Sermon on the Mount."

Seeking to remedy this sad state of affairs, we've been working our way through the Sermon on the Mount, specifically the Beatitudes. It is God's desire to temper our lives by his spirit and character as revealed in Christ's life and message.

We arrive now at the fifth beatitude. "Blessed are the merciful, for they shall obtain mercy."

What It Means

In the Greek *mercy* is *eleos*, meaning "compassion." The word is *chesedh* in Hebrew, meaning "to sympathize, to feel what others feel."

Mercy is not a wave of pity leading to "Aw, tough luck!" followed by a quick hug and the thought, "Whew! Thank God it's not me!"

When Queen Victoria's husband, Prince Albert, died she was left quite lonely. Her good friend Mrs. Tulloch lost her husband also. The queen paid her a surprise visit, and when she was announced, found Mrs. Tulloch resting on the sofa. The widow rose hastily to dress, but the queen insisted, "No, no! This is not a royal visit from the queen. It is a visit from one lady who has lost her husband to another." That's mercy. Compassion ... sympathy ... feeling the pain another feels. It is getting outside yourself, your plans and feelings, and experiencing the life of another.

Isn't this what God did in the incarnation? Job asks, "Hast thou eyes of flesh? Dost thou see as man sees?" (Job 10:4). In Jesus Christ the answer is a resounding "Yes!" Christ felt the hunger and fed the multitudes. He felt the leprosy and healed. He felt the grief of a widow now bereft also of her son, and raised the dead. He felt the lost's agony and sought them like a shepherd does his wayward sheep. And he even encouraged us to do the same in his parable of the Good Samaritan.

Such sympathizing compassion is difficult to achieve, for we're each so absorbed with our own feelings, schedules and personal problems, that it's very difficult to recognize there are, indeed, others around with needs also. Consider Martha's story in Luke 10:38-42. Jesus is but a few days from his death and he knows it. So the master retires to Bethany, the home of his good friends Lazarus, Mary and Martha. He just wants to rest, to snare a few hours of peace from the hectic pace of ministry. Martha misreads Christ's needs, instead becoming overwhelmed in her own. The Lord is her houseguest. She must play the gracious host. She must live up to her reputation as a good cook. She must entertain!

But all Jesus desires are a nap, peace and quiet, listening ears. Yet he has to contend with Martha's hustle and bustle and complaints.

Still today, when one visits a sick friend in the hospital, it is easy to stay too long, talk about one's own aches and pains, and meet one's own needs while missing those of the ill friend.

I've a friend in ministry who lost his son in a car crash. "You'll never know," he says. "Fourteen years ago ... it still hurts so bad!" In his church last year another couple's son was killed in a car accident. The pastor visited. The father saw him coming and ran out the back door. The minister followed. The father, shedding hot tears of anger and grief, began to run. For over two hours in a cold, windy rain, the father walked and ran, the minister trailing him. Finally the dad stopped and allowed the minister to catch up. He had no words. The two simply embraced in the shivering cold and began to walk home together.

"Oh, the blessed fulfillment of the merciful, the compassionate, those who can feel the pain others have. They shall obtain mercy themselves."

That is something of what the fifth beatitude means.

The Mercy-To-Us, Mercy-From-Us Principle

The first four beatitudes prepare me for the fifth. I recognize my spiritual poverty and am poor. I mourn. And I'm meek. Thus, when God offers me his righteousness, I go after it with intense hunger.

Now, as a recipient of grace, I immediately run into other people. And guess what? They are sinners just like me. But will I give grace to them even as I've received it myself? The fifth beatitude teaches that one must be prepared to offer others the same mercy God has given them.

This "get/give mercy principle" is not isolated in Matthew 5:7. One finds it later in the Sermon on the Mount, specifically in the Lord's Prayer. "And forgive us our debts as we forgive our debtors" (Matthew 6:12).

In Matthew 18:23 and following, Jesus told a parable about what happens when we refuse to be merciful. A man who owed the king millions of dollars was told to settle his account. When the debtor begged for more time, the sovereign had mercy on him and forgave the debt. Whereupon the forgiven man went out, found a fellow who owed him a measly $20, seized him by the throat, and demanded payment. When the man couldn't pay he had him put in debtor's prison. Word of this reached the king. And he got mad! He had the unforgiving man arrested and put in jail to be tortured. "I forgave you. Should you not yourself be forgiving?" the king asked. And Jesus drove his point home: "So shall my heavenly father do to you if you do not forgive your brother from your heart."

So there you have it! "The mercy-to-us/mercy-from us rule." Mercy in. Mercy out. Or we become clogged. We become a stagnant pool.

See this spiritual principle at work in King David's life. In middle age, a brooding, lonely David spied Bathsheba immodestly bathing atop her house. "Yes, here is a worthy conquest for a man of your talents!" Satan soothed. So David sent for her. She came. And there was adultery.

When Bathsheba became pregnant, David panicked and had her husband slain. He married the woman and for a year went about his business as if he'd done nothing wrong.

Covetousness, adultery, murder, and lying — four of the ten commandments fell like dominoes. Then the prophet came. And David did not once seek to justify himself. Psalm 51 is his prayer of penitence. And God offered him mercy (2 Samuel 11-12).

Now turn to 2 Samuel 9 and see how David who knew how to receive mercy also knew how to give mercy. One day David recalled his friend Jonathan, his loyalty, his servant's heart. And David mourned Jonathan's death in battle. Wondering if any of his friend's family still survived, David investigated. And sure enough there was a son — Mephibosheth. But he lived in hiding and, due to a terrible accident, was crippled in his feet.

Think of it! Mephibosheth, once a prince in line for the throne, was now hiding in fear of the new king. He was too crippled to work effectively. He had no pension, no hope. One might say Mephibosheth was in the same shape physically that David was in spiritually.

And David offered him mercy. He called him out of hiding, gave him a place at his table, and treated him with dignity. So you see, as David received mercy so he gave mercy.

This same principle must work in our lives as well. I must be meek because I am a sinner. But I must be merciful because others are sinners.

There is a wee poem I breathe daily. It goes:

"I never go out to meet a new day,
Without first asking God as I kneel down to pray,
To give me the grace and tolerance to be,
As patient of others as He is to me."

Some Examples

What have we seen so far? We have seen that mercy is sympathetic compassion, the ability to feel what others feel and touch their need. We have seen that mercy received means we become a conduit of mercy to others. Now, some examples of this mercy in action.

In the early years of the twentieth century the German Albert Schweitzer was a world-class organist, the foremost interpreter of Bach. He was also a renowned theologian, author of the acclaimed *Quest for the Historical Jesus*. But at age 40 he was also a medical doctor. And he left the comfort of Europe for the hurts of Africa, founding Lambrini, a Christian medical mission. There he treated the lame, the burned, the wounded and the fevered. As his patients began to recover, Schweitzer would lean over their beds and whisper, "The reason you have no more pain is because the Lord Jesus Christ told the doctor and his wife to come to Africa to help you ...."

Ernest Gordon fought in Burma during World War II. When the Japanese overran Allied forces there, he, along with thousands of other soldiers, was put to forced labor on the Burma Road. The Japanese relished cruelty. As prisoners suffered hunger, fatigue and jungle fever, many grew too weak to work. They were rifle-butted, even bayoneted. All this while the Japanese ate and drank in front of them.

Late in the war, however, the Allies reversed the fortunes of war. Prisoners were released and put on trains for the coast. Japanese soldiers were captured and herded into prison camps. Gordon, in his book, *Through the Valley of the Kwai*, recounts how his train stopped to take on water and coal. Men got out to stretch their legs. And there by the tracks, languishing in the tropical sun, was a group of wounded Japanese soldiers. A few of the G.I.'s shared their water and food with them and began to treat the wounded.

Though the Japanese had not been merciful, a few G.I.'s decided it had to start somewhere. And they'd be the ones to begin.

Then there is Martin Luther King, Jr. At the height of his nonviolent 1960s civil rights campaign for black equality, it was brought to his attention that a trusted aide was embezzling funds. What to do? If the press got wind of it, the scandal would injure his credibility. Other aides counselled harshness. "Expose the man and ruin him," they advised. King asked for a night to think it over and next day announced, "No. We're not going to ruin him. The world has enough examples of ruin. We shall give them an example of redemption." And that aide went on to repent and prove his worth.

A few years ago I was preaching in Camden, South Carolina. To clear my head I'd taken a walk through the village cemetery. An odd grave marker caught my eye. It read, "Sergeant Richard Kirkland, the angel of Marye's Heights." It seems during the Civil War battle of Fredericksburg, Virginia, that the rebels had hidden behind a stone wall and let the Yankees come to them. A huge massacre of bluecoats resulted, over 12,600 Northern casualties. The dead and wounded covered acres of ground in the chill of December. The killing fields writhed in agony, men calling for help, begging for water, for a blanket. No one moved to help, afraid of snipers. That's when a Southern soldier in his early twenties left his rifle pit and went to aid the wounded. From his selfless efforts he earned the sobriquet, "the angel of Marye's Heights." Sgt. Kirkland was later killed in action at the battle of Chickamauga in Georgia.

In Bangladesh last year catastrophic floods swept away the lives and livelihoods of thousands. Christians moved in to help without regard to caste or religion. They provided food, shelter, and love. Today, as a direct result of such mercy, over 2,000 Hindu families are enrolled in a Bible course considering the claims of Jesus Christ.

At a church I once served in Virginia some prison guards on a hot summer day rested their work gang on the lawn in the shade. I invited the men to use the ice water fountain and rest rooms inside. They took advantage of this hospitality for several weeks. However, at the next elders meeting there was a complaint about how it looked for such criminals to be using church property. After ten minutes of intense debate, a wise elder put an end to the matter by quoting Jesus: "For as much as you have done it to the least of these, my brethren, you have done it unto me."

Conclusion

So, here we are seven verses into the mere 107 verses of the Lord's Sermon on the Mount. And it is life changing! Church changing! City changing! Even world changing! For, indeed, nothing quite changes us like mercy.

At a local high school, Bruce, a 17-year-old, was asked as a part of a Fellowship of Christian Athletes Bible study to provide early morning transportation for a seven-year-old boy to and from a hospital for treatment. He didn't want to do it, for it meant getting up at 6 a.m., picking the boy up at 7, and having them both back at school by 8:30. But he'd agreed when the faculty adviser pointed out the family's lack of a car and the child's serious need of treatment.

Bleary-eyed from the early hour, he'd pulled in front of the boy's house, opened the door, and accepted the teary-eyed mother's thankfulness. Kid beside him, he'd pulled into traffic and sped toward the clinic. From the corner of his eye he could see the lad watching him intently. Finally the child asked, "Mister, do you work for God?" Bruce replied, "I'm afraid not, little fellow! Why do you ask?" The child explained that last night he'd heard his mother praying, asking God to send one of his workers to help him get to the doctor. "So that's why I asked you if you worked for God."

Bruce hung his head. He held back the tears. And finally he said a prayer, "God, I haven't worked for you very much. But from now on I want to do so more and more!"

"O *the blessedness* of the merciful, the sympathetic and compassionate. They shall receive mercy themselves."

Give me mercy, Lord, that I may pass it on.
In Christ's name. Amen.

7

The Bliss Of The Clean Heart

Blessed are the pure in heart, for they shall see God
— Matthew 5:8

Oliver Wendell Holmes wrote, "Now and then men's minds and hearts are stretched by a new idea and never shrink back to their original dimensions." Certainly the Sermon on the Mount is such an idea. And certainly our lives are being stretched never to be the same again.

We come now to the sixth beatitude, "Blessed are the pure in heart, for they shall see God."

What It Means

The Greek word for *pure* is *katharos.* We get our name Kathryn from it. Besides being a wonderful name, *katharos* has several uses.

It can mean "clean," as in "Are the clothes clean?"

It can mean "sifted," as in "Has this wheat been winnowed?"

It can even mean "purged," as in "Has this army unit been purged of all cowardly and ineffective soldiers?"

It can mean "unmixed," as in "This wine hasn't been watered down, has it?"

And, finally, *katharos* can also mean "unalloyed," as in "This ring is pure gold. It has not been alloyed with any other metal."

So, what does the sixth beatitude mean? "O the bliss, the blessed fulfillment of the pure, the clean of heart, those unalloyed ...."

It is a fair question to ask what it means to be "pure *of heart*." The Greek word for heart is *kardia* which means "the middle," or "the thoughts and feelings and will of a human." Simply put, the heart is the center of one's personality.

Hence, the purity Jesus is speaking of is not so much the outer cleanliness of a scrubbed face, clean hands and feet. Rather, it is the inner cleanliness of thoughts, motives and feelings.

As an example, consider the Pharisees of Jesus' day. They dressed with ceremonial appropriateness, ritually washed their faces and hands, and extraordinarily performed every religious rite — fasting, tithing, praying, praising. Yet in Luke 11:39 Jesus criticized these Pharisees harshly, "You make clean the outside of the cup, but your inward part is full of extortion and wickedness."

You see, it's rather easy to look religious by getting dressed up, taking a seat on a pew, being baptized, having your name on a church roll and mouthing a hymn. But while one sits there looking pious, one can be brimming full of jealousy, lust, pride, and anger.

Martin Luther wrote, "Christ wants to have the heart pure, though outwardly the person may be a drudge in the kitchen, black, sooty, grimy, doing all sorts of dirty work."

So, "blessed are the pure in heart ..., fulfilled are the clean, the unalloyed, the sifted, the purged ... blessed are these pure, not just on the surface, but inside as well."

That is something of what this beatitude means. Now this ...

The Trouble With Purity

Sigmund Freud, the father of modern psychology, taught that there are only two motives: sex and money.

If in your busy week you will pause and inquire of yourself, "Why am I doing this?" you will surely find you have some hope for financial gain or you are flirting so as to be thought clever, attractive, and even desirable sexually. Truly these two motives lurk in the shadows of the human heart, motivating what we do. Oh, we may deceive ourselves, veneer our motives with pious talk, but as the prophet Jeremiah observed, "The heart is deceitful above all else, and desperately corrupt. Who can know it?" (Jeremiah 17:9).

In 1971 I visited the Soviet Union. While in Leningrad I found an old Christian cathedral now housing a museum of atheism. Inside was chronicled every failure, every sham, every loveless deed of Christendom. I'll never forget holding a lovely crucifix, golden and bejeweled. The curator smiled and said, "Nice, isn't it? But push this button and see what happens!" I did and to my horror, a dagger blade shot forth from the bottom of the cross. Such is the human heart.

Several years ago, at the height of the televangelists' sex and money scandals, Skip Stogsdill and I interviewed Billy Graham at the Grove Park Inn in Asheville, North Carolina. "How do you stay pure, Mr. Graham?" we inquired. "I constantly run scared," the great evangelist confessed. "Why, I can look in my life and see the depths of hell." And so can we all, if we're honest. For ever since the fall, sin has reigned, bringing every sort of base motive, falsehood and ravening wolflike desire within.

But now this!

How To Achieve Purity Of Motives

A hard-bitten American businessman watched a

young and pretty Christian nurse clean a man's gangrenous leg. The puss and odor were utterly revolting and the man exclaimed, "I wouldn't do that for a million dollars!" The nurse looked up, met his eye, and quietly spoke, "I wouldn't either. But I *will* do it for Jesus."

Obviously there are other possible motives beside sex and money. True, the unregenerate may be pushed and pulled by a chaos of urges all centering around money and sex. But for the regenerate, the born-again, the spirit-filled Christian, there is the fact of a new heart and a new motivation.

I call it "The most amazing picture of the twentieth century." It is the photograph of a man in a South African hospital. He is sitting up in bed, holding a jar in his hands, and looking at his own heart! The man had received a heart transplant so now he was examining his old, diseased one.

In the Scriptures we are told our old *kardia* is sin diseased. There is no purity in it. It is turned to stone before God. Yet our Lord Jesus, the great physician, can perform spiritual surgery on us, take out our old heart, and give us a new one. In Ezekiel 11:19 God promises, "I will give them an undivided heart and put a new spirit in them; I will remove from them their heart of stone and give them a heart of flesh."

Once any of us has received this spiritual transplant a whole new array of motives comes into play. One may observe this in First and Second Corinthians. The apostle Paul had gone to Corinth to minister. And he found it one tough city! They criticized his preaching, did not respect his authority, refused to pay him, infighting broke out among the congregation, and drunkenness and sexual immorality were apparent.

Any time you think your church has problems just go read Corinthians!

The question is, why would a man of Paul's caliber tough it out among the Corinthians? It certainly wasn't for sex or money! This is why it is so exciting to read the letters Paul wrote to the Corinthians. They are among his most intensely personal epistles. It is as if Paul takes the top off his head and lets you look inside. For there you can discern his motives.

In 1 Corinthians 15:11-21, Paul writes about the motivating power of love. "For the love of Christ constrains us." Elsewhere he mentions the motivating power of gratitude, duty, hope, beauty, reward and faithfulness. Then in 2 Corinthians 5:11, he mentions fear as a motivation. "Therefore, knowing the fear of God, we persuade men."

There is fear that debilitates; these are your basic human phobias. But there is fear that facilitates, the sort of fear related to awe, respect, and reverence. The facilitating fear is what Paul is talking about. It is the fear of the Lord!

I'll never forget taking my son Bryan with me to a university debate on abortions. I was representing the pro-life point of view while my worthy opponent took the pro-abortion position.

I was nervous. The feminist I was to debate was polished, intelligent, and wily.

I arrived three hours early, went over my reams of notes, prayed feverently, couldn't eat, and paced in a garden. All the while my 12-year-old son tagged along. Finally, Bryan looked me squarely in the eye and said, "You're scared, aren't you, Dad?" I told him I was. "But what are you scared of?" he pushed. I confessed I was scared I wouldn't do a good job. I was frightened my opponent would make me look silly.

"Then why didn't you just stay home?" he asked. And he reminded me my favorite television show was airing at that very hour.

I grew quiet for some time. And when finally I spoke again, I had the answer from my own heart, a new motivation Christ himself had put there. "I am afraid, Son. Fearful of being unprepared, of being made to look silly in front of hundreds of students, but most of all I fear God. What will his judgment be for our nation when we sit back and allow over a million babies a year to be slaughtered by abortion?"

So you see, God can take away our impure motives and replace them with love, reverence, a sense of beauty, faithfulness, hope, heavenly reward. As Jesus himself said, "Out of the heart flow streams of living water!"

Conclusion

You will notice in the sixth beatitude that the Lord offers a reward for the pure in heart. This is the case with every beatitude. For the poor in spirit there is the kingdom of heaven. For the mournful, comfort. For the meek, an inheritance of the earth. For the hungry and thirsty, satisfaction. For the merciful, mercy. But for the pure in heart, there is the most special gift of all! "They shall see God!"

Think of it! We shall behold the Creator, the Almighty God, Ancient of days. The indescribable Holy One in whose heart was born the divine redeeming strategy of the incarnation, the cross, the resurrection, and the indwelling fullness of His Spirit. We shall see him! And that will forever be enough!

Lord, take my diseased heart and give me yours
that my motives might be pure.
For Christ's sake. Amen.

8

Peacemaking: The Seventh Beatitude

Blessed are the peacemakers, for they shall be called sons of God — Matthew 5:9

In a Charles Schulz *Peanuts* comic strip, Lucy tells Charlie Brown, "If I were in charge of the world, I'd change everything . . . And I'd start with you!" Isn't that just like us? But the beatitudes focus on one's own self. "Let's begin with you," God says.

And so we move to the seventh beatitude of Jesus. "Blessed are the peacemakers, for they shall be called sons of God."

What It Means

In the Greek *peacemaker* is *eirene* which simply means "peacemaker." But in Hebrew the root word for peacemaker is *shaloam*, a word rich in meaning. Shaloam-peace is never just negative, as in the absence of trouble or war. It is also the presence of everything which makes for someone's highest good.

A common misunderstanding of the seventh beatitude is the notion that it says, "Blessed are the peace-*lovers*. . . ." Some there are who love peace so much they go along to get along, refuse to make waves, settle for peace at any price, evade the issues. To have peace they become appeasers. But Jesus warned, "Do not suppose that I have come to bring peace to the earth. I did not come to bring peace but a sword" (Matthew 10:34). So we are to be more than peace*lovers*. We're called to peace-*making*.

As an example of peacemaking, consider a common pot of violets on your household windowsill. A bit parched, starting to brown, they haven't bloomed in two years. So you determine to be a peacemaker for them.

First you have to take away harmful things. A dog chews on them. Kids knock the pot off the sill. It's too cold or too hot where it sits. So you remove these threats. But you still haven't created shaloam.

For you must add the presence of helpful things. Sunlight in the correct amount. Moisture. Fertilizer. Pruning. And in four months the pot of violets is a verdant, blooming beauty. You were a successful peacemaker.

Saint Augustine defined peace as "the tranquility of order." It is the absence of things hurtful, the presence of things helpful. And it is not something we only strive to do for houseplants, it is something we do for people.

Historically, this beatitude has been understood several ways.

The early fathers believed it meant making peace within their own souls. Each of us is a veritable civil war walking around battling within such foes as anger, bitterness, worry, jealousy, doubts, hate and other unsettling passions. Being a peacemaker means starting with yourself. So many of our early fathers of the faith joined a monastery and in a life of quiet reflection built peace. "The peace of God, which passes all understanding, will keep your hearts and your minds in Christ Jesus" (Philippians 4:7).

Others believe peacemaking is spiritual peace best achieved through evangelism. Romans 5:1 says, "Since we are justified by faith, we have peace with God through our Lord Jesus Christ."

C. S. Lewis observed, "Man is not only a sinner who needs to be saved, he is a rebel who needs to lay down his arms." You see, the entire human race is at war with God and we shall certainly be brought to bay and held accountable for our sinful deeds by an almighty, holy God.

Peacemaking then can be proclaiming the reconciliation and mercy God holds out in Jesus Christ. It is calling people to repentance and faith and a life of loving fellowship with God. This is spiritual peacemaking.

Still others understand being a peacemaker as creating sociological peace. It is working to make the world a better place, to establish justice, to cause quarreling to cease, to right wrongs, to establish right relationships with people.

During the Civil War, president Abraham Lincoln wrote, "Die when I may, I would like it said of me that I always pulled up a weed and planted a flower where I thought a flower would grow."

So will the real peacemaker please stand up? Is he spiritual? Sociological? Or psychological? The answer is: All of them together ... and more!

You see, peacemaking is ministry. It is anything that contributes to human wholeness, be it educational, psychological, sociological, political, ecological, or spiritual. In 1 Thessalonians 5:23, Paul wrote, "May God himself, the God of *peace*, sanctify you through and through; may your whole spirit, soul and body be kept ...." See here how God cares for the whole person?

You will pardon me if I tell an indelicate story, but it serves well to prove my point. I was traveling through eastern North Carolina to a remote college where I was to preach in chapel. I'd been on the road for three hours and needed to find a rest room. Mile after mile passed with nothing but swamps and fields, and I was getting desperate! You can imagine my relief when I rounded a curve and saw Piney Woods Baptist Church building with a "Visitors Welcome" sign out front. I pulled up and ran up to the door just as a deacon came out. "Please," I said, "may I use your bathroom?" He looked at me aggravatedly and said, "Well, I don't know! Are you a member here?" Without replying I pushed my way inside and found what I needed. As I left the old gentleman was still standing on the steps looking ill.

But shouldn't the church as peacemaker meet all of our needs? Bible study and friendship, emotional health and discipline, prayer and accountability, physical healing as well as missions?

Kodak Moments

That is something of what peacemaking means. Now this: Some examples of making peace. I call them "Kodak moments."

In the 1960s, civil rights activist Dr. Martin Luther King, Jr., encouraged blacks to put away violence as a tool to achieve goals. All the while Black Panthers and Malcolm X were encouraging violence. King wrote, "The ultimate weakness of violence is that it is a descending spiral, begetting the very thing it seeks to destroy. Instead of diminishing evil, it multiplies it. Through violence you murder the hater, but you do not murder hate."

Dr. King tested his theory in his march on Selma, Alabama. He and his freedom marchers, hundreds of them, met the local sheriff at the Selma bridge. Told to disperse, King replied they had a valid permit. The sheriff sent in the dogs and billy-clubbing police. It was a very good place for a race war to begin. But King and his marchers simply absorbed the blows and did not resist. All the while the news cameras rolled. I watched it all on the evening news as a young teenager, and understood even then who had won.

O the blessedness of the racial peacemakers, for they shall be called the sons of God!

In Rochester, Minnesota, a new church was struggling to be born. Over the years a fellowship of enough people to really begin to get things done came together. But there suddenly rose a divisive issue that split the church right down the middle. Tempers flared, there was nit-picking and ugliness. Finally one group left to form another church.

The remaining elders talked things over and decided no issue that divided them was all that important. The fight was mostly personality conflicts. So they all resigned and the remaining church went and joined the other group!

The other group was suspicious at first, and didn't want to receive the second group. But with humility and acts of servanthood this group began to win their way.

Three years later, the new elders of the church told the former elders, "Now that we've been leaders for some time, we see how hard it must have been for you. Please forgive us for our surliness and division."

O the blessedness of peacemakers in the house of Jesus Christ, for they, indeed, shall be called children of God!

Now go with me to a U.S. aircraft carrier in the Pacific. The time? World War II. Max was a young sailor caught up in war. One of the boys, he was out for a good time. In his berthing area was Henry, the only Christian in the squad. And Henry was the brunt of every joke. He was cursed, mocked, ignored, and just about anything else the enlistees could think of.

Every day Max watched as Henry read his Bible and knelt to pray. The men threw their shoes at him. Henry quietly polished them. He was the only berth mate who did not gamble, read pornography, and constantly quarrel. And if you asked Henry about his faith, he quietly and patiently explained things. Max watched Henry's life for six months and secretly admired him.

Then came a great naval battle and Japanese kamikaze pilots turned the U.S. carrier into an inferno. The warship was barely afloat. Max fought fires for 48 hours nonstop. The dead were stacked in a hangar below deck. And the sailors finally took a break for food and rest. That's when Max noticed Henry was missing.

He searched for him among the living. He sought him among the dead. And the next day he found Henry in the hangar under several corpses. Henry had been left for dead, horribly burned. He'd taken whole pages from his pocket Bible and torn them out, clutching them to his chest. Max tried to console him, gave him a sip of water, and just before he died, Henry told Max, "Tell my parents I fought the best I could, that I loved Christ to the end. And, Max — tell my parents not to hate the Japanese."

For Max Scranton that day started a search for the God who could help a man love like that. And it ended with faith in Jesus Christ, a call to the ministry, and Max's having no small impact on my own life.

O the blessedness of the peacemakers who lead others to know Jesus Christ!

Still another Kodak moment came in the mid-1970s with Black tennis star Arthur Ashe. He was winning a match in a national tournament, but his opponent was being immature, abusive, and profane. Ashe, always well-mannered and cool, watched his losing opponent throw his racket down in unsportsmanlike conduct again, so he walked over to the referee and told him he was quitting the match before he lost his own temper.

The referee was stunned. It meant Ashe would forfeit the match even though he was winning! But Ashe did it anyhow.

Later the U.S. Tennis Association awarded Ashe the "win" and fined his opponent for his unsportsmanlike behavior. Such was the courage of Arthur Ashe to make peace, to be a positive role model for youth.

I could go on and tell you of parents peacemaking with their children, of divorcees learning to make peace with their ex-spouses, of employees holding their corporation accountable. But you get the picture!

In 1938, Italy's dictator Benito Mussolini told his people, "War puts the stamp of nobility on a people who have the courage to meet it." How like us. But how unlike Christ.

Jesus said the outcome of his grace working within us is not hostility, jealousy and injury. It is peacemaking. The stamp of divinity is to help bring the sinful chaos of life within and without into the tranquility of divine order.

My, but how the world tries to make peace! We've the League of Nations, the United Nations, treaties and nonaggression pacts. It seems like there is always a peace conference going on. But two problems chronically arise: first, too much talk and too little action; and second, we leave God out of the peace. And it is forever true that we cannot achieve the brotherhood of man without the fatherhood of God.

Galatians 5:22 points out that peace is a fruit of God's indwelling Spirit. It is the result of following Christ. It is neither self-generated nor politically conjured.

In the early 1930s a Protestant missionary to Japan wrote a terse letter to his church. In it he observed, "Japanese society is becoming militant by the day. Either send me 10,000 missionaries now to teach Christ's love or send me a million of your sons in ten years to fight them in war." To a world still so spiritually in arrears, his words still ring sorrowfully true.

Conclusion

As we conclude, be aware of the reward for peace-making. "Blessed are the peacemakers, for they shall be called the sons of God."

In the Greek "called" means "owned." God "owns" the peacemaker as his very son. "This is my beloved son in whom I am well pleased!"

"Sons of God" is a Jewish manner of speech. In Acts, Barnabas is called a "son of encouragement." It is a Hebraic way of saying Barnabas was an encouraging man. Likewise, Jesus is the "son of man," or fully human, incarnate. So in the text to be a "son of God" means to be doing a Godlike work.

What does the seventh beatitude mean? "Blessed . . . fulfilled . . . doing what God created you to do . . . blissful is the man who is a peacemaker, who brings people together . . . . Happy is the man who creates a nourishing atmosphere that leads to spiritual, psychological, and social peace. He shall be owned by God for he is doing a Godlike work."

Lord, help me to make peace,
for Jesus' sake. Amen.

9

The Bliss Of The Martyr's Way

Blessed are those who are persecuted because of righteousness, for theirs is the kingdom of heaven. Blessed are you when people insult you and say all kinds of evil against you because of me. Rejoice and be glad, because great is your reward in heaven, for in the same way they persecuted the prophets who were before you — Matthew 5:10-12

In the beatitudes Jesus says a Christian's pilgrimage is much like climbing up one side of a mountain and then descending the other side. One begins with a sense of his own abject spiritual poverty before God. Then he learns to care, to grieve over sin. Next he is meek, filled with humility. Finally, the Christian reaches the peak of the mountain he has hungered and thirsted to attain. And he is satisfied.

But God will not allow us to sit upon the heights savoring our relationship with him alone. He directs us down the other side of the mountain. Hence the next four beatitudes deal specifically with our relationship with people. The first step down is mercy. As I have myself received mercy, I am urged to offer mercy to others. Next my motives are called into question. Are they pure? Downward I climb to be a peacemaker, to be a nurturer. And finally I come all the way down among sinful humanity to where I am persecuted. The thanks I get for my trouble to be merciful, pure, and a peacemaker is to be misunderstood, slandered, rejected, imprisoned, and perhaps slain.

The eighth beatitude is the odd one in that it is not a description of some positive character trait found in a Christian. It is rather a description of the likely outcome of living the Christian life: suffering at the hands of people.

Ah, but one must marvel at the sheer honesty of Jesus Christ. Today, many preachers tell us that if we believe in Jesus our sins will not only be forgiven, but we'll become a king's kid — prosperous, never sick, always loved and appreciated. But this is not what Jesus told the twelve at their ordination. Quite the opposite! Our Lord said we'd be "reviled," "persecuted," and victimized by people "uttering all kinds of evil against" us.

This is not exactly a popular message to preach. But Jesus is honest. He tells us up front what to expect. And that is that the Christian life is not only hard, it is unpopular and will likely get you in at least as much trouble as it will get you out of in this life! So all through our life with Christ, we must remember that God is not so much interested in making us comfortable as he is in making us holy.

With this in mind, let's take the last step off the mountain down into the eighth beatitude and see what is there for us.

What Is Persecution?

In the Greek *persecution* means "to pursue," "to press toward." Hence, persecution means pressure. Three words or phrases in the text aptly describe it: "revile," "persecute," and "utter all kinds of evil against you." What Jesus is saying is this: "If you live with the character of these beatitudes forming in your person you can reasonably expect society to put you under pressure.

Persecution takes various forms. It can be verbal: "all kinds of evil uttered against you!"

Early Christians were slandered by outsiders who believed they were cannibals and given to sexual orgies. Since they met in secret, ate the Lord's supper as Christ's body and blood, and were so affectionate with one another, it is easy to see how such talk got started.

Still today Christians are victimized by the lies and slander of the human tongue. Just look how believers are portrayed in mass media as ignorant, intolerant, easily led, no fun, hypocritical, and having a low view of women.

Persecution can surpass mere talk. It can be economic. A certain early Christian stonemason was offered a contract to build a pagan temple. He needed the work. But there was a conflict between his faith and his business interests. He laid the problem before his pastor and concluded with the remark, "What can I do? I must live!" "Must you?" asked the pastor.

It is the same today with Christian doctors and nurses called upon to perform abortions, Christian grocers pressed to stay open on the Lord's Day, a quick market clerk asked to sell pornography, or a waitress asked to dress in a suggestive manner and serve plenty of alcoholic beverages to lusty clients.

Sometimes a Christian must say no and suffer the economic consequences.

Persecution can also take the form of social pressure.

In the ancient world, most parties were held in pagan temples. An invitation might read, "I invite you to dine with me at the table of our lord Serapis." A lamb was killed with a small portion burned to their god. A part was given to the priests. Then the rest was eaten at a dinner party. The whole affair began with a prayer to idols and a cup of wine poured out to Serapis.

Christians could not participate in such affairs. So all too often their social life dried up and they became lonely and ostracized.

Family pain is yet another form persecution takes. Often a man became a Christian but his wife did not. So a religious division developed in the household. Thus values, holidays, and worship became a source of contention.

How often I have watched young men and women at college convert to Christ, spend a year growing up, and go home over the summer to mildly religious parents who scorn their newfound faith.

Persecution can also become political in nature. When the Christian church was young, the Roman Empire was experiencing disunity. The emperors tried to use religion, specifically emperor worship, to unify the nation. It became law that each citizen must pledge his first allegiance to the state. The image of Caesar was set up in each town and once a year each person must stand before it, burn a pinch of incense and bow down saying, "Caesar is lord!" Having done so he was given a certificate allowing him to buy and sell as a loyal Roman citizen.

For Christians such an act was a defilement. Only Jesus is Lord. So they went without the certificate and were thus considered outlaws. Many were hunted down and killed. Others were thrown to the lions as sport in the arena. Others were wrapped in oily rags and used as human torches in Nero's palace gardens.

And it is very possible that we shall see such terror rear its ugly head again in our generation.

What, then, is persecution? It is pressure brought to bear on Christians that is meant to hinder or destroy. It can be verbal, social, economic, even political.

Where Does Persecution Originate?

Some persecution comes from outside the church.

In 286 A.D. Emperor Maximan of Rome ordered the army to take part in a pagan sacrifice and then assist in purging Christianity from Gaul. A certain legion of over 600,000 soldiers, all Christians, refused. The emperor ordered a decimation. Every tenth man was killed — over 60,000 men! The rest of the army stood by Jesus. A second decimation was ordered. The rest of the army stood firm in the faith. So Emperor Maximan ordered the entire legion slaughtered.

Persecution almost invariably arises from people who have something to lose. In this case it was an egomaniacal emperor who refused to allow any God but himself.

But persecution does not just come from outside the church. Often as not, it originates inside the church. Jesus' worst tormentors were religious Pharisees. And if you study church history there is a corrupt and bloody side to it that is most depressing. As it usually happens, the church slides into corruption and ineffectiveness. A reformer steps forward. There is a response of jealousy, anger, and a panic attempt to maintain one's own position. Then the persecution starts.

During the English Reformation, Thomas Cranmer set out to cleanse the church in Great Britain by calling her back to the Bible. He was arrested and tortured, and eventually recanted. For his signature on a document denouncing his reform efforts, he was given his freedom. He shortly came to his senses, reannounced his reforms, and was rearrested and burned at the stake. As he faced death he said, "Now I come to that which troubles my life more than anything that I ever did or said in my whole life, and that is that through fear of death I signed with my hand what I do not believe in my heart.

When I come to the fire, this hand shall be the first to burn." Thomas Cranmer went to the stake smiling. When the fire leaped up, he held his right hand in the flame until it was burned away.

Let's face it: whether persecution comes from inside the church or outside, it is Satan who inspires it. For the devil has hated Jesus, his words, and his people from the start. And he'd like nothing more than to destroy it.

Why Does Persecution Come?

This eighth beatitude is often grossly misunderstood. It doesn't say, "Blessed are the persecuted." It says, "Blessed are those who are persecuted because of righteousness." You see, this beatitude gives Christians no license to be dumb, to go "asking for it," to be immature, to be ill-tempered and rude, or even to do something wrong.

Too often Christians call persecution down on their own heads. Because of self-righteous and objectionable behavior we deserve the pain we receive! I well recall a group of high school students who sat proudly in the center of the school cafeteria and both prayed and read Scripture loudly. You can imagine the rest of the students' reaction . . . Persecution!

This beatitude says we're blessed when we so become like Jesus that persons take offense at us. Jesus said, "If the world hates you, know that it hated me before it hated you. If you were of the world, the world would love its own; but because you are not of the world, therefore the world hates you. Remember the word that I said unto you, the servant is not greater than his lord. If they have persecuted me, they will also persecute you" (John 15:18-20).

Never forget that people tried to stone Christ, to throw him over a cliff. He was rejected in his hometown, a murderer was chosen over him, a friend betrayed him, and he was executed on a cross. All this and Jesus said we could expect more of the same. He said, "You will be hated by all nations for my name's sake" (Matthew 24:9). He even said there'd come a day when people kill Christians and think they've done God a favor!

So our persecution should never be because we are immature or guilty of wrongdoing, but because we are like Jesus, the result of a clash between two irreconcilable kingdoms, two different value systems. And we become a threat to the sinful way things are.

How Do We Respond?

So far we've asked of persecution: What is it? Where does it come from? Why does it come? Now, we must inquire: How do I respond to persecution?

None of us wants to be hurt, rejected, tormented, misunderstood, or jailed. When we are, what's our reaction?

Some opt for avoidance, wallowing in the fear of involvement. I like the cartoon that has a Roman Christian being led out to the lions in the arena. "Okay," he says to the guards, "I'll admit to being a Christian. But I never served on any boards or anything like that."

Shame is another response. "I must be a bad person if this is happening to me."

Then there is anger at God. "I deserve better than this. What sort of father are you if you can't take any better care of your children?"

I could go on chronicling pity, depression, and all manner of retaliation. But the text says our response should be to "rejoice and be exceedingly glad." In the Greek it means "to leap up exceedingly high for joy!"

Why?

"For so men persecuted the prophets before you," Jesus said. In the early church, to suffer for Christ was considered a privilege, a badge of honor which men like David, Noah, Gideon, Elijah, Stephen, Paul and Jesus wore.

Polycarp, the 86-year-old leader of the early Turkish church, was arrested for being a Christian. He was given the choice to worship Caesar and live, or profess Jesus and die. "Eighty and six years have I served Christ and he has done me no wrong. How can I blaspheme my king who saved me?" So he was burned at the stake. His last prayer? "I thank thee that thou has graciously thought me worthy of this hour."

Jesus said we could also rejoice because "great is your reward in heaven." This world is not all there is. For there is an afterlife, a heaven, a paradise with Christ. One may take my life, my car, my job, my loved ones, my reputation, my money, but no one can rob me of Jesus and my reward. "For me to live is Christ, to die is gain."

Another reason we can rejoice in our persecution is that by our struggles we can make things better for those who follow. There is a World War II soldiers' cemetery in England. The gate sign reads, "Remember all you who pass by, we gave our tomorrows for your todays." Certainly there are sacrifices, hurts, and forfeitures any Christian worth his salt must offer up to Christ these days. But why? Why? The answer is: we do it for our children and our grandchildren.

Yet another cause to leap for joy in our trials and tribulations is because of how such pressure forms our character. In 1 Peter 1:7 our persecutions are described as trial by fire. But in Malachi 3:2 God says he is Lord of the refiner's fire. I have ventured to Israel and seen the street vendors who take silver coins, melt them in their small fire pots and refine them into jewelry. Every few minutes the silversmith will look into his pot and take a spoon and skim the impurities off the top. He knows his silver is pure when he can see his face in the molten silver.

Likewise God uses pain, the furnace of affliction, to refine us. How does he know when we are done? When he can see himself in us.

Stand Tall And Straight!

The eighth beatitude is the longest of them all, and the only one with a commentary attached. This one is simply so hard it has to be explained.

Notice that the eighth beatitude is uttered in the third person to people in general. But the commentary is uttered in the second person. It is specifically directed to the disciples, as it is now to you and to me so directed.

Strange to go from peacemaking to persecution. But Jesus is saying if we live like him the world will certainly recoil in hostility simply because our life is a public rebuke to sin.

Over the last 96 years there have been so many martyrs. In fact, more Christians have been killed in the last 96 years than in all the former 1,900 years put together. And it is predicted by church experts that the next four years will see more persecution than ever before.

Steel yourselves. Settle it in your minds beforehand. You will suffer for the faith.

Peter wrote, "Don't be surprised at the fiery ordeal that is coming upon you as if something strange is happening to you . . ." (1 Peter 4:12). Jesus has warned us beforehand.

Those who've survived years of torture in prisoner of war camps say the worst pain doesn't come from beatings, starvation, or brainwashing. The torture that breaks a man quickest is a prison cell so small that a man must crouch; he cannot rise to his full height.

Jesus is telling the church to stand up tall and straight! For such are the times that would pressure us to stoop . . . .

Jesus, you are God the Lord of me.
Help me to stand up tall and straight
for you this hour. Amen.